P9-DBP-518

obsessive-compulsive
disorder

Sandra Giddens

ROSEN
PUBLISHING®
New York

Published in 2009 by The Rosen Publishing Group, Inc.
29 East 21st Street, New York, NY 10010

Copyright © 2009 by The Rosen Publishing Group, Inc.

First Edition

Library of Congress Cataloging-in-Publication Data

Giddens, Sandra.
Obsessive-compulsive disorder / Sandra Giddens.—1st ed.
     p. cm.—(Teen mental health)
Includes index.
ISBN-13: 978-1-4042-1801-7 (library binding)
1. Obsessive-compulsive disorder. 2. Obsessive-compulsive disorder in adolescence. I. Title.
RC533.G53 2008
616.85'227—dc22

                                                    2008010902

Manufactured in the United States of America

contents

chapter one

What Is Obsessive-Compulsive Disorder?

*G*abriel is a talented artist. He can draw anything and plays a number of musical instruments.

He can't really explain why, but Gabriel has to arrange and rearrange things over and over. Everything in his room is organized "perfectly," which means the books are flawlessly aligned on the shelf, the hangers in his closet are exactly two inches apart, and his music collection is ordered by color and alphabetically.

Gabriel also feels like he has to do things in fours. He eats everything four at a time— four bites of hamburger, *then four fries, then four sips of soda. He taps each doorway he passes through four times. And he buttons and unbuttons his shirt four times each morning.*

He knows his behavior is senseless, but he can't stop himself. Gabriel has Obsessive Compulsive Disorder.

—"Get Smart About OCD," Obsessive Compulsive Foundation of Metropolitan Chicago

As a teenager, it is normal for you to feel bored sometimes with your life. You may see yourself following the same routine over and over again: going to school, coming home, eating dinner, and doing homework. The good thing is that you always know that you can break up the boredom by participating in sports, attending family functions, going to parties, and taking part in school events. For some teens, their lives are a series of endless routines filled with behaviors they feel compelled to repeat time and time again. It's not boredom for these teens. It is obsessive-compulsive disorder (OCD).

OCD is a neurological disorder in which obsessions and/or compulsions are present. OCD is characterized by recurring, unwelcome, and disturbing thoughts (obsessions) and repetitive, ritualistic behaviors (compulsions) that people with this disorder feel driven to perform. About one million teens in the United States suffer from OCD. They have fears and anxieties that they cannot seem to control. It's as if their brain gets stuck on a certain thought and replays itself in an endless loop. To help relieve their anxiety and nervousness they commit repetitive behaviors. These thoughts and behaviors usually interfere with their day-to-day functioning. Furthermore, many teens living

Many teens are embarrassed by their OCD and try to hide its symptoms. Others are frightened by their compulsions and obsessions and exhaust themselves constantly fighting them.

with OCD do not go for help or treatment as they see their condition as embarrassing and, therefore, try to hide it.

If you suffer from OCD symptoms, the earlier you seek support, the better you will feel.

A Common Disorder

OCD is the fourth most common neuropsychiatric illness in the United States. Currently one in two hundred children and adolescents have OCD in the United States, and one in forty adults have it. More than three million Americans suffer from OCD. About 90 percent of people with this anxiety disorder have both obsessions and compulsions, with approximately two-thirds reporting more than one obsession. OCD tends to develop earlier in boys than in girls. In younger children, boys with OCD symptoms outnumber girls three to two. Though the symptoms of OCD can appear in childhood, people usually do not receive a diagnosis until they are older, either in their adolescence or even as an adult. When it comes to teens and adults the ratio of men to women with OCD is about equal. OCD affects both men and women.

There are generally two peak ages for the onset of OCD, the first being in the pre-adolescence years between ten to twelve, and the second being during early adulthood from twenty to thirty years old. If the onset is in childhood or adolescence, the illness can persist through to adulthood. In fact, among adults with OCD, one-third to one-half developed the disorder during childhood or adolescence. Girls have more washing compulsions, and boys have more checking compulsions. Most people with OCD know that their obsessions and compulsions make no sense, and they are embarrassed by them, but they can't ignore or stop them.

Obsessions

Obsessions are ideas, images, and impulses that run through a person's mind over and over again. You may know that these thoughts are disturbing and irrational but some-how you think you can't control them. Obsessions often produce a great amount of anxiety. For example, you may have reoccurring doubts that

Compulsive hand-washing and obsession with hygiene are very common manifestations of OCD.

you turned the stove off so you might check the stove over and over again to ensure that it is off, throughout the day. The thought that the stove was not turned off is the obsession, and the checking behavior is the compulsion.

Compulsions

People who have OCD react to their overwhelming anxiety with repetitive behaviors called compulsions. For example, if you have obsessive thoughts about germs, you may spend hours and hours repeatedly washing your hands. Performing this behavior makes the anxious feelings go away for a short time, but when the nervousness comes back you will repeat this routine again many more times. In some young children, the compulsive behaviors occur without the previous appearance of obsessive thoughts. Surrendering to compulsions tends to make the obsessions worse, especially over the long run.

One of the worst parts of having OCD is that you know that your obsessions and compulsions are irrational, that they do not make sense, yet you experience difficulties in controlling them.

Here is a brief look at the chain of obsessions and compulsions:

- Something in your inner or outer world triggers an obsession.
- The obsession manifests itself in a ritual.
- The ritual triggers relief.
- The cycle ends.
- The cycle starts again.

chapter two

What Are the Signs and Symptoms of OCD?

Y ou might be a perfectionist, wanting to do everything just right and holding yourself to a very high standard of performance in everything you undertake. This does not necessarily mean that you have obsessive-compulsive disorder (OCD).

Do you constantly wash your hands nonstop throughout the day until they are raw and chapped? Do you constantly check to see if the door is locked? Do you line things up on your desk and cannot deal with anyone moving an item out of place? Are you constantly requesting

Many people with OCD are compulsive checkers. Before leaving the house, they may repeatedly check to make sure locks are secured, the stove is off, and windows are closed. This ritualized process can take hours.

family members to repeat strange phrases or engaging in answering the same questions? Do you have a persistent fear of illness or feel that something terrible will happen? Are you reluctant to leave the house at the same time as other members of the family? Do you wipe off doorknobs in your house after people touch them? Are you unable to control your runaway thoughts? Do you feel that you must perform rituals over and over?

All these may indicate that you suffer from obsessive-compulsive disorder. Symptoms of OCD can start any time, in childhood, adolescence, or adulthood. The symptoms can either appear suddenly or gradually. Without getting help and treatment, OCD symptoms can vary in intensity over time and for some they can even worsen.

It might be hard for your parents to recognize your or your sibling's OCD because children and teens may become adept at hiding OCD behaviors. They may think that the ritual is a phase their child is going through and will eventually outgrow.

Common Behaviors

Common Obsessions

- Constantly checking that appliances have been turned off
- Being compelled to confess or tell something
- Fears of causing oneself or others harm
- Fears of acting on violent or aggressive impulses
- Fears of losing control
- Fear of contamination, infection, and germs

- Sexual thoughts
- Disgust with bodily waste or fluids
- Fear of thinking sinful or evil thoughts

Common Compulsions

- Excessively checking appliances to make sure that they are turned off
- Excessively checking that doors are locked
- Counting (i.e., counting in groups of four, arranging objects into groups of five, taking the same number of steps to get to your desk from the classroom door each time)
- Needing to follow a set route when traveling
- Setting up your personal items in a certain way (perfectly aligning objects at right angles)
- Excessive washing (particularly hand-washing or bathing)
- Hoarding (like saving newspapers and not throwing them out)
- Excessively cleaning

Many people have unique obsessions that can't be easily characterized. Even frequently occurring obsessions and compulsions have unique features that can also vary from person to person. Regardless, obsessions are about something that is highly unlikely or impossible, yet it provokes fear, and compulsions are in response to these obsessions. They can be excessive or inappropriate mental or physical actions that temporarily reduce the fear.

Common Obsessions and Their Related Compulsions

Common Obsessions	Related Compulsions
Fear of harm or danger	Checking
Constant and severe anxiety	Ordering
Fear of contamination/germs	Washing and cleaning
Fear of loss	Hoarding
Fear of violating religious rules (blasphemy)	Praying
Morbid thoughts of sex or harm	Avoidance
Body-related obsessions	Grooming
Need for symmetry	Arranging
Perfectionist obsessions	Need for vocal approval

People with checking behaviors are plagued with doubts, or reoccurring thoughts, about safety. Checking means constantly needing to reassure yourself that you have done a certain task by repeatedly looking to see if your stove is turned off or your door is locked, for example. The obsessions that motivate this behavior can be from:

- An irrational fear of harm resulting from your error
- Concerns over imperfections
- Incompleteness

For a number of people suffering from this compulsion, they can suffer from self-blame or self-criticism for imagined negligence even though they are more careful than most other people. Many obsessions come with some form of checking. Sometimes people with checking compulsions can develop rituals. For example, you feel the need to check that the stove is turned off, so you count six steps from the stove to the door and six steps from the door to the sidewalk. Eventually, you need to do both the checking and the six steps all the time. The ritual is designed to ease your mind of anxiety but in fact becomes a self-perpetuating engine of that anxiety.

The need to arrange your environment "just so" and the feeling of intense anxiety when anything is out of place is a strong indicator of obsessive-compulsive disorder.

Ordering

Ordering obsession is the need to put everything in the exact same place. Many times it is an effort to relieve anxiety or combat anxious thoughts by arranging certain items in a set order. For example, your desk must have everything in a certain order and in place, and you can't deviate from that arrangement. You must arrange the items in your cupboard according to color. These obsessions may have started because of fear that if it is not just so, something bad will happen. It may be difficult for you to have people in your room because if they rearrange your items, you may find it difficult to cope. As soon as they leave, you will be compelled to put everything back the way it was.

Washing and Cleaning

Washing obsession is one that you see portrayed many times in films and books about OCD. Many times it is an unfounded fear of contracting a dreadful illness or disease. Many people who have washing compulsions may have had a frightening experience associated with contamination that created their fears. You might feel the need to wash your hands excessively, in a particular way or a number of times to ensure cleanliness. Similar obsessions are related to contamination by germs, body fluids, or dirt.

Hoarding

Hoarding is the act of accumulating lots of things that you do not necessarily need or use, such as old newspapers, magazines, cans, or useless trash. The main focus for you is that you can't throw things away because of the fear that you'll want these items in the future. You may experience an uncanny attachment, and you may feel like the items have become a part of you. Throwing these things away means throwing a little of your soul or life away. Keeping and collecting certain objects gives you a false sense of security and well-being, as if walling yourself in against a hostile world or guarding against shortage and loss.

Repetitive tics, such as the need to touch certain things again and again, are a coping mechanism for OCD sufferers who gain a very temporary sense of order, control, and calm by indulging their compulsions.

Repeating or Touching

You may have the overwhelming feeling that you must touch something or repeat a behavior in order to feel right. You may do these behaviors to prevent bad thoughts from occurring. For example, you need to touch a doorframe before entering a room. You feel the need to reread or rewrite words or phrases repeatedly.

Mental Rituals

Mental rituals are purposeful, voluntary thoughts that help to reassure you or to reduce your anxiety. Some of these are:

- Counting
- Special words
- Prayers
- Imagining the opposite of the obsession (e.g., I will not hurt the person)
- Replaying a conversation in your head over and over again
- Arguing with yourself over some issue
- Fantasizing (e.g., wishing for a world without death and being caught up with the thought that people should not die)

These mental rituals can occur in response to any obsession. They are mostly connected with thoughts that are unacceptable concerning sexual, aggressive, or sacrilegious themes. Blasphemous obsessions tend to occur with people who are very religious. Mental compulsions of praying nonstop are common attempts people make to deal with these blasphemous obsessions.

Harm Obsessions

Harm obsessions involve having thoughts, impulses, or images in your mind of hurting others. For example, constantly thinking you are truly going to turn into a vampire and attack others is a harm obsession. When these thoughts are in your head, you will try and replace them with a good thought. You may turn lights on and off, tap an object, or count as your compulsion.

Sexual Obsessions

Sexual obsessions are unwanted and persistent thoughts, images, or impulses of engaging in inappropriate sexual activities. You might not allow people into your room because you feel you will not be able to control your sexual urges toward them. Constantly seeking reassurance is a common compulsion if you suffer from sexual obsessions. It is important to know that a person with OCD who has sexual fantasies is not a sex offender. The person with OCD does not usually commit an immoral or criminal act, but he or she often fears doing the act.

chapter three

What Are the Causes of OCD?

Even though obsessive-compulsive disorder is common, little is known about what actually causes the disorder. OCD has no specific cause, and there is no known OCD gene. Very few people can look back in their history and pinpoint a certain event that caused their OCD. Research has not identified any childhood experiences or parental practices that usually result in the development of OCD.

People with OCD do appear to have more activity in the area of the brain that plays the role

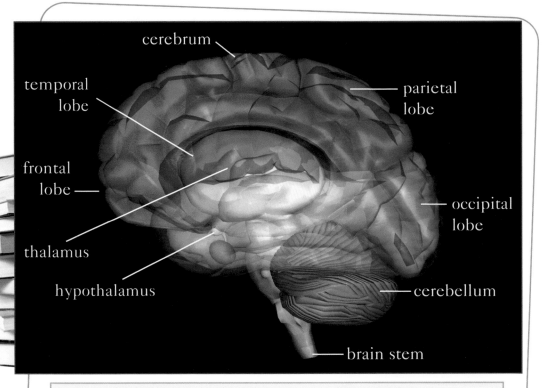

cerebrum

temporal lobe

parietal lobe

frontal lobe

occipital lobe

thalamus

hypothalamus

cerebellum

brain stem

Research indicates that OCD may be related to a communication problem between the frontal lobe and the thalamus. The thalamus may become hyperactive and send "worry signals" to the frontal lobe, despite attempts by the frontal lobe to send evidence indicating there is no cause for worry.

of allowing a person to stop or inhibit behaviors. It is unknown if this is a cause or a symptom of OCD. There are several theories about the causes of OCD.

Serotonin

Current research indicates that there might be a communication problem between the frontal lobe of the brain and the inner part of the brain. These areas of the brain use serotonin to communicate. This chemical carries messages between brain cells. In people with obsessive-compulsive disorder, there are lower levels of serotonin. Low levels of serotonin may cause obsessions and compulsions. Sometimes, by increasing the serotonin levels through medication, there can be an improvement in OCD symptoms.

Strep Infection

In some children, OCD symptoms emerge or are worsened during cases of strep throat. It is possible that the antibodies that are trying to fight the strep infection may also attack nerve tissues in the basal ganglia, which is located in the central part of the brain. This results in OCD and possibly the development of tic symptoms. Antistrep medications or antibiotics have shown some improvement in the symptoms. If you get a strep throat, don't worry that your infection will lead to OCD. In most cases, that does not happen.

Genetics

A person's risk of developing OCD is higher if one or more of his or her parents or family members already have OCD. Also, with identical twins, the frequency of OCD occurring in each twin is two times greater than OCD occurring in two nonidentical twins. At this point in time there does not appear to be a set of genes responsible for this disorder.

Possible Factors

In an effort to identify specific biological factors of OCD, brain-imaging studies have been conducted. People with OCD show abnormal neurochemical activity in regions known to play a role in certain neurological disorders. The findings suggest that these areas may be crucial in the origins of OCD. Recent studies also revealed that people with OCD had significantly less white matter in their brains, which is responsible for transmitting information.

There may also be some environmental or experiential causes of OCD. In a study at the University of California, Los Angeles (UCLA), 30 percent of the people with chronic OCD had been victims of sexual, physical, or psychological trauma.

chapter four

What Are Some Related Disorders?

Cases of obsessive-compulsive disorder have been described since the fourteenth century. Those who had obsessive thoughts in those days were thought to be possessed by the devil. Exorcism or banishing the devil from the person was the so-called cure. In the early 1900s, the psychologist Sigmund Freud thought that obsessive-compulsive behavior was due to unconscious conflicts that manifested into symptoms. In the late twentieth century there came a

In the pre-modern era, OCD was often diagnosed as demon possession and "treated" with exorcism—the banishing of evil spirits by spiritual authority.

broader understanding of the illness, as brain-imaging techniques and better research tools became available. Historically, OCD was considered to be rare, but now it is more common than other mental illnesses such as bipolar disorder and schizophrenia.

Anxiety Disorder

Anxiety disorder is one of the most common childhood disorders and is characterized by excessive fears, worries, or uneasiness. Modern psychiatry classifies OCD as one of the anxiety disorders. Some of the other anxiety disorders include:

- **Phobia.** An unrealistic, overwhelming fear of an object or situation.
- **Generalized anxiety disorder.** An excessive, overwhelming worry not caused by any recent experience.
- **Panic disorder.** Involves overwhelming panic attacks that result in rapid heartbeat, dizziness, and/or physical symptoms.

- **Social phobia.** A common anxiety disorder among teens, social phobia (social anxiety disorder) is the fear of being embarrassed by a social situation. People suffering from social anxiety disorder may blush, get the shakes, and feel nauseated when they have to answer a question in class, for example, and they worry about it all the time.
- **Post-traumatic stress disorder.** Refers to flashbacks and other symptoms resulting from a psychologically distressing event such as physical or sexual abuse, exposure to violence, or experiencing a natural disaster.

Associated Disorders

Sometimes people with OCD can suffer from related disorders, such as depression, substance abuse, attention deficit disorder (ADD), or another of the anxiety disorders mentioned above.

Many people become clinically depressed due to OCD. Once OCD is treated, the depression usually lessens. Those who are severely depressed may need to have their

Without professional help, OCD can make you feel isolated from your peers, socially anxious, and depressed.

depression treated before they get their OCD treated. Those who have other anxiety disorders as well as OCD are usually responsive to behavior therapy.

OCD in children and adolescents has been associated with motor tics and Tourette's syndrome (TS). Tourette's syndrome is a neurological disorder characterized by tics, which are involuntary, rapid, sudden movements that occur repeatedly in the same way. Research shows that 50 to 60 percent of people with TS also have OCD. Tic disorders often resemble OCD symptoms. There are differences between those with only OCD and those with OCD and Tourette's. Specifically, people with both OCD and Tourette's tend to have more touching, counting, and blinking compulsions than those with only OCD. There are also different, more successful treatments for those who have both OCD and Tourette's. People who have Asperger's syndrome, a form of autism, may also experience OCD symptoms.

When there are additional related disorders, treatment can take time, but there are specialists who are trained to help you through the process.

MYTHS AND FACTS

Myth: Obsessive-compulsive disorder (OCD) is a rare problem.

Fact: OCD is not rare. More than three million Americans have OCD. Many people with OCD often are too ashamed to get help, and they sometimes have the illness for years before seeking help.

Myth: OCD is a condition that is best treated by "pulling yourself together."

Fact: People with OCD need to get help from professionals for their illness. For people with OCD, it is not easy conquering the disease on their own. OCD is best treated by therapy and medication.

Myth: OCD is caused only by stress or worry.

Fact: At this point in time, researchers do not know what causes OCD. The disorder does have a tendency to resurface when someone is feeling stressed, anxious, or worried, but there is reason to think that biological, neurological, and environmental factors may play major roles in its development.

Myth: People with OCD are just being careful or fussy, and their problem is that they are fixated only on cleanliness.

Fact: OCD feels unpleasant and unhelpful to people who have it. They get no pleasure from their repeated actions, rituals, and constant thoughts. People with OCD are not mere perfectionists. They have an anxiety-related disorder whose symptoms they can't control. Although there are many OCD sufferers who are fixated on cleanliness, a lot of people suffer from many different obsessions and compulsions.

Myth: OCD does not start as a child.

Fact: Symptoms of OCD can start anytime, in childhood, adolescence, or adulthood.

chapter five

How Is OCD Diagnosed?

There is no X-ray or scan that can determine if you have obsessive-compulsive disorder. To receive the diagnosis of OCD, you must have obsessions and/or compulsions that cause you anxiety or distress and cannot be attributed to another cause like drug dependency. (Abuse of stimulants such as amphetamine and cocaine may induce repetitive behaviors that resemble the rituals of OCD.) For a diagnosis, your obsessions and/or compulsions must consume an hour or more of your time each day and must be disruptive to your life. If the person recognizes that the impulses, thoughts, and images he or she has are self-created or are excessive or unreasonable, or if a person tries to ignore or suppress thoughts and impulses, then those are also signs of OCD.

It is important to find a specialist who is qualified in treating OCD. You could first start with your family doctor to obtain a referral to a specialist in the field. The specialist could be a psychiatrist, psychologist, licensed clinical social worker, or

Speaking regularly to a qualified mental health professional will greatly ease your burden and eventually help reduce or even eliminate your OCD symptoms.

medical doctor. If you are having difficulties finding a good and qualified specialist, you may want to call a teaching center connected to a medical school's department of psychiatry or a university's department of psychology.

You can also contact the Obsessive Compulsive Foundation (http://www.ocfoundation.org; (203) 878-5669), which keeps up-to-date listings of OCD specialists and clinics throughout the world. When dealing with a specialist, it is imperative that you connect positively with him or her. If you have joined an OCD support group, it is also important that you feel comfortable taking a risk in talking about how you are feeling. If your parents have a medical plan, you will need to find out if the specialist or group will be covered. If they are not covered, you will need to make sure some member of the family will pay for the costs. Some specialists have sliding fees and some agencies can help you if you cannot afford to get the help you need.

Ten Great Questions to Ask Your Therapist

1. Do you specialize in teens who have obsessive-compulsive disorder? What can I expect from working with you?

2. Will you do an assessment on me? Is there a questionnaire I need to fill out?

3. What treatment do you recommend for my OCD? What is your therapeutic approach?

4. What is your fee?

5. Do you also prescribe medication?

6. How many sessions do you think I will need before I start seeing some improvement?

7. Do you have any literature, CDs, Web sites, or films you recommend on OCD?

8. Will my family be involved in the treatment? Will I have individual sessions or be part of a group?

9. If I am feeling stressed or nervous, would I be able to call you or another place for immediate help?

10. Do you have a success story about somebody with OCD?

chapter six

What Are the Treatments for OCD?

Living with obsessive-compulsive disorder can be especially hard on you. It can get in the way of having fun, doing schoolwork, and developing and keeping relationships with friends. It can also affect the dynamics in your family. If not treated appropriately, or not at all, OCD is usually chronic. In some cases it remains under control, and in others it can become disabling, sometimes even requiring hospitalization. While there is no cure as of yet, the good news is that there are treatments that can help most people reduce their symptoms or even eliminate most or all of them. About 80 percent of people with OCD will not get better without help, which means that the symptoms do not just disappear on their own. There are two forms of common treatments: cognitive behavior therapy (CBT) and antidepressant medications.

Cognitive Behavior Therapy

CBT should always be considered in treatment for OCD on its own or in conjunction with medication. CBT is a safe and effective treatment for all ages. It is considered the most successful treatment for people with OCD.

CBT is built on the assumption that a person's thoughts and feelings are interconnected, and he or she can create positive outcomes from his or her beliefs. CBT might sound scary, but it can also be empowering to realize that a person can create his or her own destiny.

The combination of medication and cognitive behavior theory yields the best results in successfully combating OCD.

CBT helps people to learn to change their thoughts and feelings by changing their behaviors. During CBT, the therapist might expose you to something you fear so that your fear is decreased.

Exposure and ritual prevention (ERP) is one type of CBT. The main focus is to decrease anxiety by exposing a person to the stimuli that causes the distress. The person undergoing ERP learns to resist the urge to engage in his or her compulsions. While exposed to his or her feared stimuli, anxiety will slowly lessen over time as the stimuli become less anxiety provoking.

While in therapy, you face situations that will have produced your obsessions and anxiety. For example, if you are afraid of germs, you might be exposed to something you consider dirty until you no longer fear it. You are encouraged to reduce, then eventually stop, performing the rituals that you think help you with your feelings of nervousness. Another technique of CBT is Socratic questioning. This is when therapists asks patients a series of questions that will force them to evaluate their beliefs. The therapist's withholding of reassurance is used with patients who constantly seek reassurance. The therapist works at trying to persuade the patient to stop seeking it.

With CBT, changes are often noticeable after eight to ten weekly sessions.

Antidepressant Medications

There is no magic pill to cure OCD, but medication is a great support for you to help in reducing the frequency of, intensity of, and distress caused by obsessions. Many of the medications help in adjusting serotonin levels in the brain. Medication seems to help the parts of the brain that deal with being able to inhibit and stop behaviors. A doctor will prescribe the medication, adjust the dosage, and monitor you for side effects. Some of the medications that are being used to treat OCD include:

- Clomipramine (brand name: Anafranil)
- Fluoxetine (brand name: Prozac)
- Sertraline (brand name: Zoloft)
- Paroxetine (brand name: Paxil)
- Fluvoxamine (brand name: Luvox)

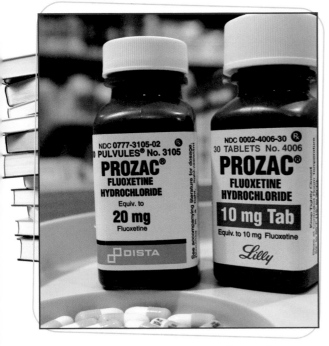

Prozac is one prescription drug that may ease OCD symptoms.

Unfortunately, taking medication usually has some side effects. Some side effects are not difficult to live with, while others make it impossible to continue taking the drugs. Side effects of a number of these drugs include dry mouth, nervousness, restlessness, nausea, diarrhea, and drowsiness. It also can take several weeks before you feel the benefits of the drugs. It can take eight to ten weeks before the medications take full effect. Your doctor may try one drug, and, if it is not achieving the results you need, will possibly recommend that you try another. Your doctor will probably start you with a small dose and gradually increase the dosage if there are no or little results. Most young people metabolize medications quickly, so relieving OCD symptoms may require more adultlike doses. To boost a drug's effect, doctors will sometimes prescribe two or more medications to be used together. Most people will respond positively to medications, but there are those who do not respond to any. Medications help to control your symptoms but they do not cure you. Drugs are constantly being tested in laboratories to see which drug or drug combination will reduce symptoms.

Combination Therapy

A study published in the October 27, 2004, issue of the *Journal of the American Medical Association* found that almost 40 percent of children receiving cognitive behavior therapy had a significant reduction in their OCD symptoms, while only about one in five children taking medication had lessened symptoms. The study found that the most effective treatment was combining the two. Almost 60 percent of those children who had combined the behavior therapy and medication went into remission.

The benefits of medication do not necessarily last after you stop taking it. For some people, medications do not help them at all, so a combination of medication and therapy still appears to be the best avenue in treating OCD.

chapter seven

How Do I Cope with OCD?

If you have obsessive-compulsive disorder, you are probably wondering if it is a good idea to keep it a secret from your peers. Each person is different. You may feel that some of your friends are empathetic and will be supportive of you. You probably also know that if people do not understand the condition, they may show their ignorance by making silly comments. If peers are willing, educating them about OCD is really half the

36

battle. Also remember OCD is only one part of you as a person, as there are many facets to your personality and life. OCD does not have to get in your way of succeeding in life. Many successful people from all walks of life have OCD and are fine, contributing members of society.

Stress does not cause OCD, but the symptoms have a tendency to resurface when you are feeling very stressed. This means if you have an event like a divorce or death in the family, a change of schools, or another upsetting event, symptoms may come back. It is important for you to learn some stress reduction techniques. These can include deep breathing, meditation, yoga, or tai chi.

Here are some things to do to take care of yourself:

- Get plenty of rest. Lack of sleep can create stress for your body. As well, if you find yourself tired and sleeping all the time, get help from a doctor.
- Eat well. It is always important to try and eat well-balanced meals and not skip meals. It is also bad for your

Since OCD can be triggered or worsened by anxiety and stress, it is important to increase your level of serenity. Meditation is a great way to do just that.

Physical health helps promote mental health. A healthy diet will do wonders for both your body and mind.

body to keep drinking a lot of caffeinated drinks such as tea, coffee, and soda. Too much junk food is also bad for your body.

- Do not try to reduce your stress by taking drugs, drinking alcohol, or taking up smoking. If you are drinking alcohol regularly, you are adding to your stress, not reducing it.
- Exercising and sports are really good for you. Exercise releases many of the chemicals found

in the medications prescribed for OCD and can be a powerful natural alternative to drugs. Try to exercise for at least twenty minutes, three times a week.

- Practice yoga. For ideas go to http://www.yogajournal.com.
- Use relaxation tapes or soothing music to help you meditate and relax.
- Make sure you do not isolate yourself. It is important that you have friends. It is also important to join clubs or participate in activities that make you feel a part of your peer group. E-mailing and being stuck in front of your computer is not getting out and being with your peer group.
- Make a list of your good points and keep adding to it. You need to see that you are worthwhile and need to appreciate your own strengths. If you keep a diary, do not dwell on the bad parts of your day.
- If you need to, remember to talk to a therapist who can help you when you are feeling very stressed.

To understand your OCD better, try to do so in a systematic manner. Here are a few suggestions of things you can do.

Find Patterns

Identify and define your compulsion by tracking cycles and patterns of what triggers your reactions, how often they occur, and what your responses are. You can do this by keeping a chart divided into three categories: before

A daily journal is a great way to get in touch with your feelings, confront your anxieties, and identify obsessive-compulsive patterns.

the compulsion, what the compulsion is, and after the compulsion. For example: feeling unclean, washing hands six times, then feeling like you can continue.

Identify Feelings

Get in touch with the specific ways in which you are feeling. See whether your feelings are accurate appraisals of situations or whether they are your usual way, or your pattern, of handling situations. This is doing a reality check.

You could also keep a journal. Try to be consistent and write in it every evening. See what has made you happy in the day, when you start feeling anxious, and when you are feeling worse. You can start seeing patterns, or you can share this with your therapist so she or he can help you interpret your feelings and develop coping mechanisms.

Become aware of your thought patterns. The more negative thoughts you have, the more negative energy you expel. How do you take negative thoughts and alter them? One way is to reframe. Is the glass half empty or is the glass half full? For example, instead of saying, "My stomach feels tight," turn it around by saying "I can relax my stomach tension by focusing inward and taking a deep breath." See what you focus on and see if you are more positive or negative. If you are more negative, see how you can work on reframing to become more positive.

Create a Support System

It is important that you do not isolate yourself. When you are feeling that you are having a bad day and your own techniques are not working, it is important to get in touch with the people who can help you. This may mean talking to your parents, a therapist, a peer, a guidance counselor, a support group, or a help line. The Internet may not be the best solution as it can further isolate you. Also, the person at the other end may not be giving you the advice you need.

When You Live with Somebody with OCD

If you live with someone who has OCD, you need to be patient with the person. Recovery rates can vary. It is important for you to praise small successes. If he or she can reduce one compulsion even a little per day, this can be a first and big step toward healing. One thing that you should not do is participate in the person's rituals. If, for example, he has cleaning rituals that cause him to take off every piece of clothing as soon as he walks in the door, you do not have to participate by immediately washing his clothes.

Another thing to keep in mind is that you are not totally responsible for the person. Do not become his or her babysitter or turn into a nag. Being up to date on the subject of OCD can only help you and the person who has this condition, so bring relevant books, CDs, and films into the home.

It is also important that you try to understand that people with OCD are not at fault for their disease. Once he or she is in therapy, it is vital that you learn to help by participating in family sessions and learning more about OCD and how you can become more supportive. Remember, each person gets better at different rates, so try to be patient and understanding.

You're Not Alone

Research is ongoing on how to treat OCD. There are new methods and medications being tried. There is no magic potion yet, but researchers continue to try and get the answers to the why's and the how's. If you have OCD, remember that you are not alone in your illness. Many people live with their symptoms every day. You can get help. Just make the call. Some immediate relief will occur when you take the first step.

anxiety A fearful physical, mental, and emotional reaction in the absence of real danger.

Asperger's syndrome A disorder most often noted during the school years, characterized by impairments in social interaction and repetitive behavior patterns.

assessment Refers to the specific instruments used to gather information.

chronic Lasting for a long period of time.

compulsion Actions a person performs, usually repeatedly, in an attempt to make an obsession go away.

depression A mood disorder characterized by unreasonable feelings of unhappiness.

gene The basic unit of inheritance in cells.

neurological Pertaining to the medical science that deals with the nervous system and disorders affecting it.

obsessions Persistent thoughts and ideas that a person cannot stop thinking about.

perfectionist Someone who is displeased with anything that is not perfect or does not meet extremely high standards.

psychologist A specialist in the scientific study of human behavior.

ritual A detailed act or series of acts carried out by an individual to relieve anxiety or to forestall the development of anxiety.

tics Involuntary, rapid movements that occur without warning.

unconscious In psychoanalytic theory, the division of the mind containing elements, such as repressed desires, that are not subject to conscious control but affect thoughts and behavior.

American Academy of Child & Adolescent Psychiatry
3615 Wisconsin Avenue NW
Washington, DC 20016-3007
(202) 966-7300
Web site: http://www.aacap.org
This nonprofit organization's Web site contains resources and information regarding young adults and mental and behavioral disorders.

Anxiety Disorders Association of America
8730 Georgia Avenue, Suite 600
Silver Spring, MD 20910
(240) 485-1001
E-mail: anxdis@adaa.com
Web site: http://www.adaa.org
This national nonprofit organization does research and advocacy and provides help for people with anxiety disorders.

National Alliance on Mental Illness (NAMI)
2107 Wilson Boulevard, Suite 300
Arlington, VA 22201-3042
(888) 999-6264
E-mail: info@nami.org
Web site: http://www.nami.org
This national organization provides support, advocacy, and education on mental health issues.

Obsessive Compulsive Information Center
Madison Institute of Medicine
7617 Mineral Point Road, Suite 300
Madison, WI 53717

(608) 827-2470
Web site: http://www.miminc.org/aboutocic.html
This Web site provides information on many mental and behavioral disorders, including OCD.

Hotlines

Kids Help Phone
(800) 668-6868
Kids Help Phone is Canada's only toll-free phone and Web counseling, referral, and information service for children and youth, providing immediate, anonymous, and confidential support, 24 hours a day, 365 days a year. It is staffed by trained professional counselors with a wide variety of backgrounds, including social work, psychology, sociology, and child and youth services.

National Institute of Mental Health (NIMH)
National Suicide Prevention Lifeline
(800) 273-TALK (273-8255)
A toll-free, 24-hour hotline that will connect you to a trained counselor at a suicide crisis center nearest you.

Web Sites

Due to the changing nature of Internet links, Rosen Publishing has developed an online list of Web sites related to the subject of this book. This site is updated regularly. Please use this link to access the list:

http://www.rosenlinks.com/tmh/ocdi

for further reading

Baer, Lee. *The Imp of the Mind*. New York, NY: Plume, 2002.

Gravitz, Herbert L. *Obsessive-Compulsive Disorder: New Help for the Family*. Santa Barbara, CA: Healing Visions Press, 2004.

Grayson, Jonathan. *Freedom from Obsessive-Compulsive Disorder: A Personalized Recovery Program for Living with Uncertainty*. New York, NY: Tarcher, 2000.

Harrar, George. *Not as Crazy as I Seem*. Boston, MA: Houghton Mifflin Company, 2003.

Hyman, Bruce M., and Cherry Pedrick. *The OCD Workbook*. 2nd edition. Oakland, CA: New Harbinger Publications, 2005.

Neziroglu, Fugen, Jerome Bubrick, and Jose A. Yaryura-Tobias. *Overcoming Compulsive Hoarding*. Oakland, CA: New Harbinger Publications, 2004.

Summers, Marc. *Everything in Its Place: My Trials and Triumphs with Obsessive Compulsive Disorder*. New York, NY: Tarcher, 2000.

Traig, Jennifer. *Devil in the Details: Scenes from an Obsessive Girlhood*. New York, NY: Little, Brown and Company, 2004.

About the Author

Dr. Sandra Giddens makes her home in Toronto, Ontario, with her husband, Owen. She is a special education consultant at the Toronto District School Board.

Photo Credits

Cover and p. 1 (top left) © www.istockphoto.com/Liv Friis-Larsen; cover and p. 1 (middle left) © www.istockphoto.com/Robert Gubbins; cover and p. 1 (bottom left), p. 25 © www.istockphoto.com/Forest Woodward; cover (foreground) © Seth Goldfarb/Photonica/Getty Images; cover (background), pp. 1, 3 (background) © www.istockphoto.com/Vasiliy Yakobchuk; p. 3 (laptop) © www.istockphoto.com/Brendon De Suza; p. 3 and additional page backgrounds (books) © www.istockphoto.com/Michal Koziarski; pp. 4, 9, 19, 23, 28, 31, 36 (head) © www.istockphoto.com; p. 4 © www.istockphoto.com/Nicholas Monu; p. 6 © www.istockphoto.com/Eric Simard; p. 7 © John Greim/Science Photo Library/Photo Researchers; p. 9 © www.istockphoto.com/Jason Lugo; pp. 10, 14 © Myrleen Ferguson Cate/PhotoEdit; p. 16 © Pinter Ginter/Science Faction/Getty Images; p. 19 © www.istockphoto.com/Quavondo Nguyen; p. 20 LifeArt Image © 2006 Lippincott Williams & Wilkins. All rights reserved.; p. 23 © www.istockphoto.com/Tracy Whiteside; p. 24 Scala/Art Resource, NY; p. 28 © www.istockphoto.com/4x6; p. 29 © Peter Berndt, M.D., P.A./Custom Medical Stock Photo; p. 31 © www.istockphoto.com/Bonnie Schupp; p. 32 © Pulse Picture Library/CMP Images/Phototake. All rights reserved.; p. 34 © Stephen Chernin/Getty Images; p. 36 Shutterstock; p. 37 © www.istockphoto.com/koch valérie; p. 38 © www.istockphoto.com/Christopher Hudson; p. 40 © www.istockphoto.com/Christine Glade.

Designer: Nelson Sá; Editor: Peter Herman
Photo Researcher: Amy Feinberg